Closing Time

Poems

Arthur Ramer

Clare Songbirds Publishing House Poetry Series
ISBN 978-1-947653-95-5
Clare Songbirds Publishing House
Closing Time © 2021 Arthur Ramer

All Rights Reserved. Permission to reprint individual poems must be obtained from the author who owns the copyright.

Printed in the United States of America
FIRST EDITION

Pen and ink drawing © 2021 Candi Ramer

Clare Songbirds Publishing House was established to provide a print forum for the creation of limited edition, fine art from poets and writers, both established and emerging. We strive to reignite and continue a tradition of quality, accessible literary arts to the national and international community of writers, and readers. Chapbook manuscripts are carefully chosen for their ability to propel the expansion of art and ideas in literary form. We provide an accessible way to promote the art of words in order to resonate with, and impact, readers not yet familiar with the siren song of poets and writers. Clare Songbirds Publishing House espouses a singular cultural development where poetry creates community and becomes commonplace in public places.

140 Cottage Street
Auburn, New York 13021
www.claresongbirdspub.com

Contents

Chance Meeting on the Road Home	9
The Chef's Coat	10
Tommy's	11
Blame Enough	12
Tommy II	13
The Last Time I Saw Lino Palacios	14
The Bank	15
Broken Mouth	17
I Imagine	18
Short Story	20
Reading Slowly	21
Ecstasy Moments	22
Two Blood Red Roses	23
For Canastota	24
Bonny Dee	26
The Hill	28
Hary's Hats	29
For Joe Ramer	36
Black Wholes	37
Never Quite Closing Time	38

The author wishes to thank Clare Songbirds for originally publishing "Short Story" in the anthology *The Brave* and to the Rip van Winkle 2008 Hudson Valley Writers Poetry contest for awarding "Never Quite Closing Time" top honors.

In Arthur's name, I dedicate this book to our dear friend Rachael Ikins, without whose drive, talent, passion and friendship this compilation would never have been completed. Times ten.

With special thanks to Matt Leone for having made it possible for Arthur to attend the Colgate Writers Conferences.

~Candi Ramer

I write my best poetry when I'm not holding a pen.

A. R. 4/22/06

Chance Meeting on the Road Home
Rachael Ikins

I met my friend Arthur
at a Writers group
in the Earlville Opera House,
2007, Earlville, a smaller town
in the middle of no where,
Upstate, New York.

He arrived late, drank
a tall cup of gas-station
coffee, read Gothic Poetry.
Talked about his wife, Candi,
his son Robert's autism.

The pink renovating house where
they live, scooped out like a soft-
boiled egg from its shell from the side
of a mountain.

He owns a sushi place,
plays harmonica since he was 11.
Carries a glass of ice-cubed vodka,
presides over incredulous students,
the rice cooker, and me.

He is the first person who
understands my Poetry
whore. He is my people.
Driving to Westchester,
tuning the radio,
looking for a poem.

How you never refuse
that whore, side-of-the-Road;
When she puts her thumb out,
When she cocks her hip.

The Chef's Coat

I'm a solitary cook.
I don't want you
In my kitchen
Unless you're walking through
Both quietly and quickly
To the bathroom
Or unless I've asked
You to join me
So we can talk while I work.
And if while there
I'm inventing
And I talk out loud
Wondering, "What if I
Combined this with that,
Over this, with caramelized that,
So that you'd have
The sweetness of that,
The saltiness of this,
With this and that…
I don't know…What do you think?"
I'm not really
Requesting a reply.
Just shut up, open your mouth
When told, and eat.
Make a noise in your throat,
Then smile.
It's all I need.
I'm a solitary cook.

Tommy's

On the back wall of Tommy's
Is a black and white picture of Leo
He ain't smiling, which is good,
'cause Leo didn't know how.

Leo was Tommy,
But Leo didn't want no one to know his name.
So he called the place Tommy's

How the hell Leo wound up in a college town
Is a mystery to everyone
Probably including the long-dead Leo.

Now Al is Tommy.
Got a wide smile that goes grim as he turns the corner.
His handshake's firm, but his hand shakes when he holds a glass.
Graduated twenty years ago with high-flying
Plans of youth

Disappointments and decades
Nailed his shoes
To the worn smooth wood
And taught him his final college town lessons

So here it is.
A tradition for all fake-ID'd freshmen,
An afternoon woodchuck hole for all alcoholic townies.
Tommy's.

Jukebox good music,
Smoky sweet bluesy.
Darklights.
Mirror reflection bottle-blocked.
Stale peanuts
Buy the taps or the first shelf booze;
The well's water'd down.
Last stool's mine.

Blame Enough

I escaped one night
By ripping tears
Out of a face
That couldn't comprehend,
That melted like mascara'd
Wax, that knew it would die
Alone, and would never
Figure out why.

So now, here's why.
It was the death of my heart
That beat until it was beaten,
Was scarred every day by scares
Real and imagined,
That huddled like a hobo
Over and oilcan fireplace to feel
The warmth the normal feel,
Yet never felt normal.

It was how I forgot
Who I was, how I chained myself
Into the game of make-believe.
I'd have done better
To rage instead of screaming full-mouthed
At my own failures.

And you're not blameless too.
My fraud was equaled
By your Cyclops blindness,
With both hands over one eye
So that you could only see what you
Wanted to see. Not once
When I stood in the night-shadowed
Backyard, in a corner, smoking
A cigarette, hiding, did you ask me
Who was the enemy, and could you
Stand with me
Against the judgers.
You were born to one of them, and I knew it.

Tommy ll

Jeanne the unknown
Stands silent, back to the bar,
Wipes glasses smudged with fingerprints and lips,

Dreams in solitude movies,
Sinks in a quicksand cage,
Refuses to reach for a hero's hand,

Will die a mystery of mute anger.

Maye is an ancient cobra
Defanged by time.
She hums lullabies
To the young she devoured.

Scours the kitchen clean,
Leans on canes that betray her evenings,
That wait by her morning bed
To mock her old age.

The Last Time I Saw Lino Palacios

The last I saw
Lino Palacios
He was boarding
An Amtrak train
From unknown Utica
To be swallowed
Into the pyrite bowels
Of Yonkers,
To bend his back
With his amigos
To scoop horse-shit forever
So as not to soil
The spoiled feet
Of the girls
Who ride gelded racehorses
Around and around
The arena.

The Bank

I could procrastinate no longer
So I called The Bank.

Laurie could no longer speak
To me.
Only Bruce could speak
To me.
Bruce must be More Important.
Laurie transferred the call.

Bruce picked up
The phone.
After quick bullshitty niceties,
Bruce asked, "Arthur, why haven't
You
Paid the car note?"

I was dumbstruck.
Why??? I thought.
(Ya know, its amazing
That in just a blink
You can think and link
A dozen thoughts.)

And what I'm thinking is…
1)"What an idiotic question!"
2)"What a f**king moron!"
3)"Well, Bruce, I was on the steps
    Of The Bank, ready,
    I swear,
    To pay the money
      When a dog came up
      And ate my homework!"
Instead…
I smiled at the phone
And said
"Well, ya know, Bruce,
I didn't have the money."
Bruce seemed surprised
By my reply's
Simplicity.

Pity
Poor Bruce
Who must listen
To every ruse
That those with pride left
Can invent.

But I
Felt freed.

Broken Mouth

I run my tongue
Over jagged shatters
That have quietly but quickly
Replaced the teeth I used to know.

They are craters
With knife-sharp ridges.
They cut me
And hurt me
And abuse all the soft
Parts of my mouth.

I am too poor
To pay for their repair,
And too prideful
To allow anyone else to.

I am broken in America.

I Imagine

I strike quite
the pose,
one foot up on the bumper
of the truck
ballcap with perfect
curved brim
old weathered jeans jacket
Marlboro smoke
a blue purple wish
shades by sunset
on the bay beach
behind me.

I imagine
If I woke my wife
Inside the truck
Looking out at me
Knowing how she loves me
She must think me
Handsome.

But when I think of this
I think of what I look like
In the morning.
Same old fuck
Sagging, jowled, grayed
Dismayed at his reflection.

If the I
In yellowed Polaroids
Passed the me as I am
The I
Would not know
Me.

I've become 55
Staring down the barrel
Of 65
(Father dead at 66)
So many days turned decades
Gone
The boy I remember
Could be my grandson

All stale
All used
All knobby
And sagged

The sunset kite soars.
How it must yearn
To catch a breeze
And fly
Unfettered.
But its tied
To its capturer
As I am tied to time.
I remember
When I could fly.
I never even felt
The string.

Short Story

I'm reading a book
Of short stories
Written thirty thousand years ago
In nineteen eighty nine.

If there are veterans,
They're dressed in jeans, wear
Beards and long
Hair, swig
Whiskey in tall glasses
And refer obliquely
To 'Nam.

I close the book
On my chest
And marvel at how many more
Vets there are now.
All in the name of God
And country, and family,
And baseball and booze.

Time has dripped away,
Wetting swamps and sands.
And I'm amazed
At how we've wasted away
The fortune of our future
Into futility.

Reading Slowly

What makes
A thought a poem?
Do you always have
to reach a point?
Come to a conclusion?
Have some cutesy way
to wink and say,
"Goodnight, folks. And thanks
for coming."?

Writing is my aggression
my warfare
my love making
my exorcism
my excusing
my reaching out
my hands in prayer
      Or in fist
my walking naked
my kneeling, bleeding
my palms cupping the water
      to let you drink.

If you're hearing this
now from my lips,
it's because I need you
to hear me.

If you're reading this…
stop.
Listen for my voice.
Now, read it again…
slowly
as if begging for forgiveness.

Read this as if each poem
was a complete confession
of sin and sacrifice.

Now
read it again…
Slowly.

Ecstasy Moments

There are moments
when I touch the ecstasy
and the pop-pop-pop
of fleety thinking
boppity jazz
stone-y as
when I was young
takes me away
and my internal syncopation
is vamping it
camping it

And I have to pull myself in
from flailing my arms
machine-gunning syllables
into the heads of
victim listeners.

Two Blood Red Roses
(For the Hokies) after the shooting at University of Virginia

two blood red roses
fell to the floor
scattering their petals in a pool.

although outside the morning was bitter
and cloudy
inside the greenhouses
the weather was warm
and life-giving.

yet even the trees
leaning against the doors
couldn't stop the storm.

and thirty other red roses
fell to the floor
and covered us all,
their petals catching on our tears
and flying into our moaning mouths
agape with sadness.

For Canastota

The men look older than me.
Thank god I can't retire.

They're dressed in plaid,
angry at the world,
bewildered at who took their history
and screwed it up.
They're pissed like righteous 15 year old's
who know *you* just don't get it.
I'd love to get drunk with 'em all,
and let the shit fly where it may.
These are not old squares,
barely able to make the stair-
way to heaven.

Christ! Is that what I'm going to become, have become?
Anarchic revolutioners won't raise clenched fist,
Arthritic panther claws can't close.

The women, mostly gray,
grandmotherly,
all have their poems stacked neatly,
like schoolteacher desks.
And yet,
I'm sure they all moaned their own
slow songs of woe
 and wonder,
lust and love.
It will be interesting
to scratch their surface.

I'm so used to reading
to the oh so shocked young
who are amazed
that I write it straight.
My paper
is a sacrificial table.
What I tell and what I know
are chained down together for the slaughter,
though my past pleads with silent eyes,
"Don't. You know how my blood
has always stained you."

But I cannot stop.
If I painted pretty things
you'd like them
and forget them.
And even I'm not sure that would be wrong.
But my demon would not
have died of exposure,
and although I know
that only death will bring closure
I keep hoping merely for pardon,
not salvation.
If death is only silence,
then I might as well scream now.

Bonny Dee

Bonny Brook Stable
Sprawls across the open
V of a valley
That wakes East in sunrise,
Rests west at its set.

It is a green-glazed goblet
Filled with
The water of a hot July sky,
The music of pine winds,
And river drums.

In the ring,
Steeled hooves dance
Light as cat paws.
Each curve-necked horse
Relents to rein
And the insistent thigh
Of Dee
Who was born between the mountains,
A glint of Norse
In her flint eye.

Watch her.
Understand why
You could hold her hand,
Yet never claim her.
There's a warrior
In the saddle
With no need
Of sword for strength.

And with each pace
Or length of leg,
Even a common ride
Turns ears forward,
Flares it's nostrils,
And strides above the dust.

The Hill

You took my window
In your hands,
Laid it down gently
On top of your mirror
And hushed me to wait
for the sun.

We waited.
Waited for the runny mud,
Waited for it to bake and crumble
Waited for the ten trillion green
Waited till we could no longer see
My window laying lazy atop
Your mirror.

In the middle of the snow field
You sat me down
On a tawny couch
Of log and brittle branches

You took my hand and led me away.
Steady up a rutted, pebbled path
Turned me
And bade me
To look now at our field below

And when the sun
Was on top of my window
That was on top of your mirror
We blazed together
In an ecstatic rectangle
Of light and heat
That seared eyes,
Sky, and memory.

Hary's Hats

At 95 and wracked with terminal everything, Hary knew it was time. He shifted painfully so that he could lie on his side and face his pudgy, middle-aged son.

"Now, Bob," Harry began, "before I tell you this, let the old man have a smoke."

Bob reached into his suit pocket, fished out a pack of Marlboros, looked past the door of his father's Fifth Avenue brownstone's bedroom to check that the nurse wasn't looking, and handed over the whole pack. "Maybe it'll kill him quicker." Bob mused.

The fact was, his dad had given him the willies since he was five, back in 1965. That was the year the family went Chapter 11, and his dad, the scion of Harry's Hats, Inc. had a nervous breakdown. The only real asset that remained was this building, bought in 1892 by his grandmother.

Hary (yes, Harry Hary. Hary's father, a stern and aloof man, had had one humorous bone in his body. Unfortunately for Harry, the joke was on him) blew out a long stream of blue 'Boro smoke.

"OK, Bob, here's what actually happened. Some, of it may seem far-fetched, but that's both the irony and glory of the Truth. Truth is weird. And Fiction made to seem like Truth has to be simple so that people won't think it's Fiction. But it's almost always the Truth that seems Fictional."

Bob interrupted. "Dad, I have to leave in a while to go get Betty from the salon, so what are you talking about?"

"Look, I don't have that much air in my lungs, so lucky you. I can't tell long stories. I'm going to tell you the facts, let you dismiss them as fancies, but at least I'll know that I did tell you before I die. So be a good boy, sit back, and shut up."

Bob sat back in his chair, glanced out the window and calculated that he wouldn't have to take too many more of these insults. Also, as sole surviving heir he could afford to be indulgent and patient.

"Sorry, Dad, please go ahead."

Harry grunted. "Yes, well, anyway...back in 1961 the hat industry began to crumble. It wasn't overseas competition. It wasn't that the Japs had figured out how to make a smarter, smaller hat. It wasn't that Hary's Hats did something stupid and the rest of the hat makers didn't.

Nope. It was the entire industry that died in one afternoon. Tens of thousands of Americans whose livelihood depended in one way or another on hats, were about to be thrown out of work because of a decision made by one man on one January 1961 afternoon. That was the afternoon that John Fitzgerald Kennedy decided not to wear a hat to his inauguration. That afternoon the American Public decided that a man not wearing a hat was a sign of virility and youth, and that wearing a hat meant that you were limp-dicked and old."

Harry took another long drag and continued. "Pretty boy flaunted his pretty boy fucking hair, and within five years there wasn't a single maker of men's hats in all of America. Even by '62 the handwriting was on the wall. We lobbied Congress and talked to some of Kennedy's inside guys. 'Let him just wear a hat to some public function' we'd say. They'd laugh and tell us 'But Jack doesn't like hats. And women voters think he's cuter without a hat.'

Then of course came the Bay of Pigs fiasco, the Cuban Missile Crisis, and the beginnings of the Viet Nam War. No one gave a shit about hats. We didn't matter to Congress. We didn't matter to Kennedy. We weren't relevant."

Harry's voice and face grew dark. "But we were relevant. We were still multi-millionaires. And we decided to protect our interests."

Slowly Harry shifted his weight again. Fucking fragile bones. "So you see, Bob, someone had to do it. Somebody was going to do it sooner or later. We just decided to kill the son of a bitch first."

Harry stopped to let his son's slow-ish brain and imagination catch up with what he'd revealed.

Soon, Bob's eyes began to twinkle faintly and then he rocked back in his chair, howling with laughter.
After he'd collected himself he said "Dad, Dad, Dad, everyone knows Kennedy was killed by the Mob or by Castro or by the CIA. But Dad, *the hat people*? The owners of Harry's Hats, Federick's Fedoras and Chez Chic Chapeaux were the real ones responsible for the greatest conspiracy in history?! I…don't… think…so! Did the doctor change your medication?" Bob shook his head, chuckling.

He stopped chuckling when Harry hit him over the head with his cane. "Bob, you're my son. I love you. But you're an idiot. We had connections with the Mob from our union contracts up north, and our felt and cloth makers down south. Not to mention the truckers and Hoffa. We knew Castro from Panama hats. Where do you think Panama hats were made? No, asshole. They made them in Cuba. Kennedy killed that trade with the embargo. And the CIA was pissed off at Kennedy after the Bay of Pigs. We just gave them all a way to piss back."

Bob couldn't believe his good fortune. If his Dad really believed this shit and told it to a doctor, then maybe Bob wouldn't have to wait for the Grim Reaper to escort Harry to the Happy Hatbox in the sky. Bob could have him declared incompetent now!

Sometimes....sometimes....not very often......Life was good.

But Bob needed a witness to this insanity.

"Nurse!" Bob shouted. A few seconds later Bob heard the nurse's footsteps coming down the hall.

"I'll need her testimony," he thought. "After that, Dad's gonna be in a rubber room hospital. I'll sell this brownstone and get at least 20 maybe 25 million. Not to mention what all of the crap in this mausoleum will bring. I can pay off Betty and finally be rid of that nagging bitch, too. And think of the possibilities then! Yeah, all of those young, tight-sweatered things that would do anything, and I mean anything, for a man with some real money!"

Bob slid the newspaper over his lap in order to hide his growing excitement as the nurse entered the room. Bob noticed that the sixty-something nurse was dressed as always, bordering on unkempt, with none of the traditional nurse trappings like a little peaked, starched white cap. "You never see nurses wearing those little caps any more." The thought passed through Bob's mind.

"Yes, Mr. Hary?" Said Nurse.

"Dad," Bob smirked, "tell the nurse what you just told me."

"O.K." Harry whispered tight-lipped. "But I don't know what the big deal is. I only asked what all that noise is outside."

Bob, annoyed at his father's lie, noticed for the first time that there was a growing crowd-type sound coming through the window. "No, Dad. Not those sounds. Tell the nurse about the hat guys and Kennedy."

"No, Son." Harry chuckled. "I didn't say Kennedy, I said 'I'd like a can of tea.' That's what your dear mother used to say as a joke for a cup of tea."

Harry smiled a "cute little old man" smile at the nurse. She turned and trudged away back down the hall.

"Doctor said you can't have tea, Mr. Hary," she called over her shoulder without looking back. And she disappeared around the hall corner.

"Dad, why did you do that? You made me look like a fool!" Bob almost shouted.

"You are a fool, Bob, " Harry snarled. "Did you really think

I'd keep a secret like the world's greatest conspiracy under my hat all these years, only to spill it in my old age to some slob nurse whose first name I don't even know? You're a bigger schmuck than I thought."

Harry grew calmer. "Now, where was I?" He continued. "Oh, yeah, like I was saying, anybody who was anybody hated Kennedy. But we were Americans. We didn't really want to fund the assassination of the president of the United States. All he had to do was wear a fucking hat for God's sake! Jackie did. She wore those little pill-box numbers. Broads were crazy for those pill-boxes. But no man would be caught dead in a hat. What was 100 per-cent was now 50 per-cent, and shrinking.

We took 5 million dollars, a great deal of money in money today, but an even greater deal of money in 1962. We went to Hoffa. Well actually, I went to Hoffa. I was always the toughest nut in the jar, and everybody, including me figured I'd be the best one to negotiate this deal.

"Jimmy," I said, " we got ourselves a common enemy. We both want him gone, and gone for good. It'll be good for us, good for you, good for the Boys. Is there a way you can think of to make him go?"

And I take a picture of JFK out of my pocket and turn it face down on Hoffa's desk. Hoffa turns it face up, leans back in his chair and whistles. His leans so far back I could see nothing but the bottom of his chin. He musta stayed that way for two minutes.

Then his head slowly comes forward. He's smiling. *Really* smiling. Like the corners of his mouth were trying to meet in the back of his head. Never saw a guy so happy. Said something like "They'll never figure out it was you guys."

Now I'm smiling. "Jimmy," I said. "Let's make it poetic."

"Whaddaya mean?" Says Hoffa.

I said "Let's make it a head shot."

Harry continued, "I reached down into my briefcase and took out the 5 mil and began to make piles on Jimmy's desk. Those days, you could still get thousand dollar bills. You know, even with thousands, 5 mil is a bunch of bundles. Must have covered half of his desk. He presses a button beneath the top. One of his bodyguards comes in through a side door with Hoffa's hat and coat. Jimmy slips them on and starts to walk out of his office. I said, " Where ya going, Jim?" He says, " Don't worry. I'm not gonna disappear. I have to make a phone-call that's best not to make here. Keep filling my desk. The green looks good with the mahogany."

"Anyway, Bob, some of the people involved are still alive so

I'm not going to mention everyone, or tell you every little detail. But I did write it all down. It's in my safe deposit box. When I'm dead, read it, burn it, piss on it, I don't care. But I know you. You'll read it. You want the money."

Harry was distracted by the growing crowd noise outside. "Bob, just what the hell is going on out there?"

Bob went to the window and looked outside after parting a pair of yellowing 19th century lace drapes.

"Just a bunch of those "Neo-Hippies " as the papers call 'em. Having a Be-in at the Sheep Meadow. I guess everything old is new again."

Bob felt his anger and disappointment at his father's "here-now, gone-now" hallucinations welling up inside of him. Finally, he blew his top.

He shouted, "Dad, I gotta tell you, this is the stupidest, most ridiculous story I've ever been told. And what's supposed to be the purpose of this farce? To make me believe it? So that in case I'm gullible enough to buy it and repeat it to someone, that you can laugh and make fun of me? Or are you trying to tell me you're sorry? That even though you and your merry band of international hat co-conspirators pulled off the murder of the century...after all that...men still don't wear hats? And that hats, like big bands, never did and never fucking will, make a comeback?

Or maybe this purpose of this fantasy is to allow you to psychologically have something that you can repent for? Well, if you're going to repent, repent for being such a failure as a father! Repent for blowing all our money. Or should I rightly say, *my money*? The money that was supposed to be *mine*. Mom told me right before she died that you blew a couple of million on some crazed scheme to try to make everything OK. And I accept that. But please, don't tell me some cockamamie story that you bought the death of John Fitzgerald Kennedy to try to save Hary's Hats!"

And with that, Bob stormed out of the door, slamming it hard behind him.

Harry just lay there for a minute, heat rising like a pot coming to a boil. In his mind thousands of pains and memories all tried at the same time to rise out of his head.

He remembered giving Kennedy a last warning at a break-fast fund-raiser that fatal November morning. A cowboy hat (an American hat. *The* American hat, goddamn it!) had been offered to Kennedy just before he left the room for the ride to the airport and plane to Dallas. Kennedy laughed, tossing it away on the table in front of him and said "I'll wear it in Washington."

The crowd laughed. The reporters laughed.
Harry, sitting in the back of the room, didn't laugh.
Thirty-five minutes later, Air Force One left for Dallas.
Thirty-give minutes later, Harry sat in a Fort Worth hotel staring at the TV, waiting for the news flash.

Harry knew, from the bottom of his heart, that someday, somebody with more brains than his son would read the safe deposit-boxed letter. Someone would begin to piece together the puzzle using the detailed information that letter contained. Details such as that Lyndon and Jackie weren't shot because they were wearing hats. But Kennedy and Connolly were hatless. That the shooter on the grassy knoll and the one in the storm sewer both wore hats.

Indeed, once you included hats as a unifying agents all the mysteries and questions surrounding the assassination were resolved.

Yes, someday they'll understand that Harry Hary, not that weasel Kennedy was the real American Hero! Harry Hary had tried to save the jobs of thousands. Thousands who would not be able to save money to buy new homes, fund their children's educations, or retire like decent human beings.

Instead Kennedy had tossed their lives, dreams, and aspirations onto some dung-heap. And why? Because some Gallup poll had shown that he looked sexier without a hat. When all was said and done, John Kennedy was just like every other politician... a bunch of ego-centric fops, sots, sluts, panderers, and philanderers.

Harry's thoughts were interrupted by the increasing commotion clamoring outside his window. He reached under his pillow, took out a flask of Jack Daniels and gulped down a very long slow slug. And then two more.

He pulled his weak legs off the bed. He grabbed his cane and hobbled over to the window. From halfway across the room he heard the crowd chant, " Harry....Harry!"

If Harry could have leapt for Joy, he would have. He had totally misread his son. Bob must have told the Neo-Hippies about what a hero his father was, and the adoring crowd was now chanting his name. There was no doubt about it. It wasn't old age or bad hearing or Jack Daniels. They were shouting at the top of their lungs, "Harry! Harry!"

Harry flung open the French doors and closed his eyes so he could feel the air and their adulation. Tears of happiness and redemption streamed down his stubbles, furrowed cheeks. He threw his cane aside and lifted his arms above his head and waved his hands furiously out the window. "Yes, Yes, it's me! Harry Hary!"

Harry's knees buckled under the excitement. He overbalanced and fell out the window like a twig to the pavement three stories below. His bare head crushed into the cement, he died instantly.

The contingent of the bald-headed Krishna Consciousness devotees who had been waiting for the light to change at the intersection below Harry's window were already moving across Fifth Avenue, chanting, "Hari. Hari. Hari. Hari Hari. Hari Krishna. Hari Hari. Hari Krishna. Hari Hari. Hari Rama. Hari Rama. Krishna Krishna. Hari Hari."

For Joe Ramer

The other evening
I said something funny
And thought my father
Would've laughed.

I tried to remember his laugh,
Yet couldn't.

I quieted my mind
And allowed it to search
Its files and long untended alleyways
Unencumbered by intent,
But my father's laugh,
Even the sound of his voice
Is gone.

I know you'll tell me
His laugh is in mine,
Or in my smile,
Or perhaps my eyes,
But I can't hear
Him anymore.

Dead before digital
And smart phones,
What I wouldn't give
To see him live
And laughing
Even if on a screen.

But like ice cream melted
on a flat plate,
It's too late.
I can pour it in my palms
And taste the sweetness
But that's as close
As I can come.

He's just a memory
Backing away
Waving goodbye.

Hey, Dad! Wait for me!
I'm coming!

Black Wholes

When it's all done
And the demons
Have stopped slinging, scourging
scythes
And the community of leaves
Have fallen to the grass
When it's all done
And the snapping traps
Echo through the valley
And the valley slams shut on itself
The Book will be closed.

Never Quite Closing Time

It's in the wet shining circle
that is miracle-floating
on top of the scattered peanut dust
strewn on the ebon wood of this bar.
It is Christ walking on the water
left by the bottom of this glass of scotch.

It's in the fleeting wry smile
that nudged the lips
of the more than middle-aged
woman sitting on the end stool
when the young girl played the same sad song
for the third time on the jukebox.

It's in the slow sway of blue-jeaned hips
that the young girl moves
with closed eyes
remembering her boyfriend
how they seemed so in one-ness
only to discover that two are two
no matter how much you make-believe.

It's in the bar rag
mopping up after another sucker leaves
more broke than buzzed.

All the wisdom of the ages is here.
You just have to know
how to look.

Arthur Ramer grew up in NYC area. His passion was the arts- music, visual art and poetry since he was a child. He moved to upstate NY and co-founded Sushi Blues & BBQs with his wife, Candi. He attended the Colgate Writers Conference multiple times. Sushi Blues hosted Monday Night Poetry at Sushi Blues, a poetry feature and open mic founded by Rachael Ikins.. He won the Hudson Valley Poetry Prize 2008. He was a member of the Earlville Writers, the Canastota Writing Group and his passion, besides poetry was mentoring students and sharing ideas. He died unexpectedly in a car accident June 21, 2013.

Author photo © John Hubbard

www.ingramcontent.com/pod-product-compliance
Lightning Source LLC
Chambersburg PA
CBHW062040120526
44592CB00035B/1801